to:

from:

reflections of the heart...

reflections of the heart...

words by Kimberly R. Rinehart

illustrations by Georgia M. Rettmer

library of congress catalog card number 87-080982

international standard book number 0-942865-01-4

manufactured in the united states of america

it takes two™, inc.

le sueur, minnesota 56058

First Printing May, 1987

Second Printing November, 1987

Third Printing August, 1988

this is your day...

to dream a brand new dream,

sing a brand new song,

touch a brand new moment

this is your day...
to be the very best
that you can be.

may you open your eyes
and your heart
to the beauty that lies
around you,

to the strength that lies
within you,

and to all that lies
before you . . .

. . . one day at a time.

not miles,
or years,

or new-found friends

will ever take away

the part of you
inside my heart

that grows...

with each new day.

for you, my friend
a gentle sigh

a heart full of moonbeams
and wings
to fly

for you,
my friend
just for you...

a field of daisies,
a sky of blue...

God loves people
who don't know how to be
anyone but themselves

that's why He made children...

. . . and that's why
He leaves a little child
in each of us.

if i could choose
a gift for you,

it would be made
out of laughter,

filled with
a song...

...and wrapped in a ribbon of rainbows

take this day...

and make of it
a joy worth living,

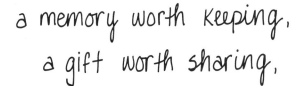

a memory worth keeping,
a gift worth sharing,

take this day...
it's yours!

i will always need
flowers
and raindrops

sunshine
and mountains

music and laughter...

. . . and a friend like you

take time to watch,
to wait, to wonder.

take time to laugh,
to cry, to remember.

take time to feel the sunshine,
take time to
touch a raindrop.

just remember. . .

. . . to take time

if you look up into
the sky at night,

and see a tiny twinkling light,

that's the star i'm wishing on . . .

. . . just for you

true love does not care
for the passing
of time . . .

. . . for time
cannot change
the true meaning
of love.

may your heart
    be always young,

may your dreams live forever...

may your spirit be free.

it's music that
stirs my heart,

it's music that
makes me
whole,

it's music that lets me dance . . .

it's music

that speaks,
when words cannot.

if you have a dream,
follow it

if you catch a dream,
nurture it

and if your dream
comes true...

celebrate it!

we have laughed together,

grown together,
   dreamed together,
you are more than just a friend . . .

you're a part of me!

remember your roots

they will give you
courage to choose your
dreams,

wisdom
to choose your path...

. . . and wings to fly.

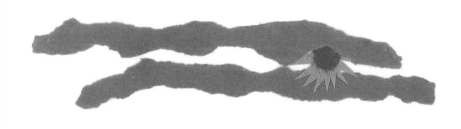

my friend,
you have given me
so much

is it any wonder
that i think of you...

... and smile

we must learn to gather
each tiny moment
of solitude and peace.

we must learn to hold them
deep in our hearts...

and remember

to touch them often.

it takes two™ is the story of a dream come true shared by the artist-writer team of Georgia Rettmer and her daughter Kimberly Rinehart. The creative effort of **it takes two**™ begins with Kimberly's gift of writing sensitive, original words that express feelings from grief to celebration. Georgia surrounds each verse with the gift of her unique, colorful torn paper art. The refreshing result is a line of greeting cards, gift enclosures, and soft-cover books that are being shared internationally by people who want to say just the right thing in a sincere, beautiful way.

Each time an **it takes two**™ card or book is given or received, our dream is shared...Each time a heart is touched or comforted, our dream lives on...

May our work find a home in your heart.

Georgia Rettmer
Kimberly Rinehart